The Star-Spangled Banner—Explained

An Illustrated Book about the Origin of Our National Anthem

Copyright © 2025 by Darryl Vidal

All rights reserved.

No part of this book may be reproduced, stored in a retrieval system, or transmitted in any form or by any means—electronic, mechanical, photocopying, recording, or otherwise—without prior written permission of the publisher, except in the case of brief quotations used in reviews or critical articles.

Illustration Disclaimer

The artwork contained in this book was created with AI-assisted illustration tools under the direction of Crane Books illustrators. These drawings are intended solely for historical and biographical purposes. Any likenesses to real individuals—many of whom are historically deceased public figures—are presented in the context of fair use for commentary and recollection.

Printed in the United States of America

Published by Crane Books – cranebooks.com

ISBN: 978-1-969705-03-8

The War of 1812

By 1812, the United States was still a very young nation—barely three decades old. Many Americans' psyches were marked and their family members lost in the Revolutionary War. Tensions with Great Britain never fully diminished. The British navy, the most powerful in the world, was at war with France, and they often treated American ships as if they were still British property.

American sailors were captured and forced into service for Britain's fleet in a practice called "impressment." This outraged the United States, which saw it as both an attack on its citizens and an insult to its sovereignty.

Another source of conflict came from the western frontier. What American's proclaimed as manifest destiny, the British saw as an unacceptable power grab by the new nation. Americans suspected Britain of supplying weapons to Native American tribes resisting U.S. expansion. British trade restrictions also hurt American merchants, who could not freely sell goods overseas.

By June 1812, sentiments both politically and in the public square were at a tipping point. In response, Congress declared war on Great Britain. Many called it "Mr. Madison's War" after President James Madison, who had reluctantly asked for the declaration, but understood their position to be untenable and unsustainable.

America on the Defensive

The early years of the war did not go well for the United States. American attempts to invade Canada failed, and British forces proved difficult to challenge. By 1814, the war had turned especially grim. In August of that year, British troops marched into Washington, D.C., and set fire to the Capitol, the Treasury, and even the President's House (later rebuilt and called the White House). The young nation's capital had been humiliated.

After burning Washington, the British turned north toward Baltimore, Maryland, which was one of America's busiest ports and home to skilled shipbuilders. If Baltimore fell, it could cripple American trade and morale. To take the city, the British needed to capture Fort McHenry, the star-shaped fort guarding Baltimore Harbor. This set the stage for one of the most dramatic moments of the war.

The Players

Francis Scott Key was not an Army general, nor a politician. He was a young lawyer from Maryland who lived a rather ordinary life until history placed him in an extraordinary moment. It wasn't even the moment itself that became the oath to our nation, although it did mark the first true test of the new nation's independence. It was his recollection of the sights, sounds and emotions of that stormy night.

Born in 1779, Key was respected in his community as a man of faith, family, and quiet dignity. He often mingled with merchants, farmers, and civic leaders in Georgetown and Baltimore, where debates about the war filled taverns and public squares.

These connections grew through his legal career, which brought him into contact with influential figures, military officers, city leaders, and, because of the proximity to Washington DC, members of the federal government.

Francis Scott Key's Mission

September 1814, Key traveled to Chesapeake Bay on a diplomatic mission. After the British burned Marlboro, some locals helped detain looters. This was deemed hostile activity towards the crown. A friend of Key's, Dr. William Beanes, had been taken prisoner by the British.

He was held on a British warship anchored in the bay. Beane's friends and neighbors feared he would be transported to England for trial, which at his age meant he would never return.

Key's sense of loyalty and honor drove him to volunteer for a dangerous mission—to negotiate the release of Beane. Francis Scott Key, along with Colonel John Skinner, arranged to negotiate for Beanes's release in advance. Surprisingly, the British agreed. Key and Colonel Skinner, sailed out to the British fleet under a flag of truce to negotiate Beanes's freedom.

It was this act of personal friendship that placed Key on a ship in Baltimore Harbor, surrounded by enemy officers, at the very moment America's fate seemed most uncertain.

However, there was one problem. While Key and Skinner were aboard the British flagship to negotiate, they overheard details of the planned attack on Baltimore. Because they now knew too much, the British would not allow them to return to shore. Instead, they were placed under guard on a truce ship, anchored several miles away in the Patapsco River.

A Night of Uncertainty

From that anchored ship, Key had a clear view of the bombardment of Fort McHenry on September 13–14, 1814. For 25 hours, British warships launched rockets and mortar shells against the fort. The sky lit up with fire and explosions, while the sound of cannon-fire thundered across the harbor. Key and his companions could see the fort but had no way of knowing what was happening inside.

If the fort surrendered, they knew the British would capture Baltimore. If the flag was torn down, it would signal defeat. But if the flag still waved in the morning, it would mean the Americans had withstood the assault. All Key could do was watch and wait through the long, terrifying night, straining his eyes for signs of the flag through bursts of red glare and smoke.

It was in those hours of suspense—unable to communicate, uncertain of the outcome—that Francis Scott Key found the inspiration for the words that would become The Star-Spangled Banner.

About this Book

The purpose of this book is to provide historical references to the most well-known national anthem in the modern world.

Even today, so many around the world don't know, never have, and never will know, or understand the concept of freedom—of life, liberty and the pursuit of happiness—as we Americans woefully take for granted.

People all over the globe have come to recognize not only the grand melody and orchestration of the anthem, but some of the most notable and relatable verses describing the new nation's war of independence from British rule and the fight for freedom, stated so succinctly in the final line of the first verse, "O're the land of the free and the home of the brave."

The Star-Spangled Banner—Explained

Line 1: "O say can you see, by the dawn's early light"

Francis Scott Key begins with a question. He is asking whether, in the first light of morning, people can still see the American flag flying. This opening line captures both suspense and hope. The night before had been filled with gunfire, explosions, and uncertainty. Key's first thought at dawn was: is the flag still there?

The "dawn's early light" isn't just a time of day—it represents survival after darkness and danger. For Americans defending Fort McHenry, dawn meant relief: they had endured the night. For Key, who had been anxiously watching, being detained on a ship in the harbor, dawn was the moment of truth.

By starting the verse with a question, Key draws the listener in. He wants us to imagine being there with him, straining our eyes in the first rays of sunlight, desperate to see if the symbol of freedom has survived.

Attack on Baltimore

Fort McHenry guarded the entrance to Baltimore Harbor. The British navy knew that to capture Baltimore, they would first need to neutralize this fort. On the night of September 13–14, 1814, the British bombarded Fort McHenry for 25 hours straight. Rockets, cannonballs, and mortars filled the sky. Key was aboard a truce ship in the Patapsco River, about eight miles away, negotiating the release of an American prisoner. Because of his position, he had a clear view of the fort and the battle but could do nothing to inform or intervene.

As the night dragged on, Key must have felt powerless. He could do nothing but watch and pray. When the firing ceased just before dawn, a tense silence followed. Would the fort surrender? Would the British flag replace the American one? As the first light of dawn broke over Baltimore Harbor, Key peered through the mist and smoke, looking anxiously for the answer.

Line 2: "What so proudly we hailed at the twilight's last gleaming"

This line reminds us of what was seen the evening before—when the sun was setting and the battle was just beginning. The defenders and observers had proudly hailed, or saluted, the American flag as it flew over the fort. At "twilight's last gleaming," the sky would have been painted with the fading colors of sunset, and the flag's stars and stripes were still visible.

The phrase also underlines the emotional attachment Americans felt toward their flag. To "hail" the flag meant more than to notice it—it meant to honor it, to feel pride in what it represented: a young nation standing up against the most powerful empire in the world.

By contrasting "twilight's last gleaming" with "dawn's early light," Key shows the passage of a single, crucial night. The suspense lies in whether what was hailed with pride at sunset could still be seen with joy at sunrise. On September 13, 1814, as twilight fell, the American garrison of about 1,000 men prepared for the British attack. The defenders were commanded

THE STAR-SPANGLED BANNER - EXPLAINED 11

by Major George Armistead. To inspire his troops, Armistead had commissioned a massive flag—measuring 30 by 42 feet—that could be seen from great distances. Major Armistead specifically asked for a flag "so large that the British will have no difficulty in seeing it from a distance." That is the flag Key describes and that was the flag he saw at dusk.

The British Fleet

The British fleet consisted of nearly 19 warships, including bomb ketches capable of hurling 200-pound mortar shells two miles. At twilight, the British began their relentless bombardment. Key, held aboard a British truce vessel under guard, had nothing to do but watch and record in his memory.

Baltimoreans also knew the importance of their city. Local geography worked in their favor: shallow waters and sunken ships blocked larger British vessels from approaching too close. But twilight marked the beginning of a dangerous night. Would the massive flag survive, or be torn down in surrender? When Key wrote "what so proudly we hailed," he was recalling that moment of shared pride—just before chaos engulfed the harbor.

Line 3: "Whose broad stripes and bright stars through the perilous fight"

Key now describes what he saw during the night itself. Despite the fierce battle, the flag's "broad stripes and bright stars" remained visible. The choice of words emphasizes both the size and clarity of the flag—it was designed to be unmistakable.

The "perilous fight" refers not just to the physical danger of cannon fire but also the uncertainty of whether America could withstand the British assault. Key's relief and amazement shine through. Even in the thick of battle, the symbol of the United States remained in view.

Key shows how a flag can represent hope in times of danger. Seeing the stars and stripes waving gave both soldiers and civilians courage to keep going, even when things looked grim.

During the bombardment, British mortars launched shells that arced high into the air before exploding. Rockets hissed across the sky. Each explosion lit up the darkness. In those flashes, Key and others could see glimpses of the flag still flying.

Geographically, Fort McHenry sat on a peninsula guarding Baltimore's inner harbor. It was star-shaped, with earth and brick walls built to withstand heavy fire. The defenders had to endure hours of incoming shells, many of which fell short into the mudflats or overshot into the water. Still, several hit the fort, causing damage and casualties. Yet throughout the peril, the flag's "broad stripes and bright stars" were never struck down.

Line 4: "O'er the ramparts we watched, were so gallantly streaming?"

Key is describing the view of the flag above the fortress walls, or ramparts. He and others watched as the flag continued to stream bravely in the wind during the attack. To "stream gallantly" suggests a bold and noble image: the flag flowing proudly, defying the enemy's attempts to silence it.

The question mark at the end of the line makes it clear Key is still anxious—he wants reassurance that the flag is truly still there. The anthem is filled with questions, reflecting his own doubt and suspense during the night.

Key reminds us that courage can be shown not just in fighting but in standing firm—like a flag waving against all odds.

What are Ramparts?

Ramparts are the protective walls of a fort. At Fort McHenry, these were reinforced with earth and stone, forming a five-pointed star shape that allowed defenders to fire in all directions. From Key's vantage point on a ship downriver, the flag flying above these ramparts was the clearest sign of whether the fort still held.

The British bombardment was meant to force the Americans to surrender. For 25 hours, the ramparts took direct hits. At one point, a shell penetrated the powder magazine (where gunpowder was stored) but did not explode—if it had, the entire fort might have been destroyed.

Despite these dangers, the defenders refused to take the flag down. In fact, when smaller storm flags were raised during the night to prevent damage, at dawn Armistead's men hoisted the massive garrison flag again. This act of defiance was exactly what Key later immortalized as "so gallantly streaming."

Line 5: "And the rocket's red glare, the bombs bursting in air,"

This line paints a vivid picture of the terrifying night. Rockets and bombs lit up the sky, each burst of light briefly revealing the flag above the fort. For Francis Scott Key, those explosions were both frightening and strangely comforting—because every time the sky lit up, he could see the American flag still flying.

The "red glare" shows the destructive firepower of the British weapons, designed to shock and demoralize. Yet in this poem, Key flips the meaning: instead of symbolizing terror, the rockets and bombs became proof that the defenders had not given up. The enemy's own firepower ended up illuminating America's resilience.

Key shows how danger can also reveal courage. What the British meant to use for fear and destruction, Key saw as a source of reassurance and inspiration.

Rockets & Bombs

The British navy was equipped with Congreve rockets—new technology at the time. They left trails of fiery red light and exploded unpredictably, creating psychological fear as much as physical damage. The "rocket's red glare" is a direct eyewitness description of what Key witnessed.

In addition, the British fired thousands of mortar shells. These "bombs" arched high into the air before exploding. The bombardment began on the afternoon of September 13 and continued for 25 straight hours. More than 1,500 shells were fired at Fort McHenry, some weighing up to 200 pounds.

Geographically, the British ships had to stay about two miles away in the Patapsco River to avoid American return fire. This distance reduced their accuracy, and many shells missed the fort. The constant booming echoed across Baltimore. Citizens in the city also stayed awake, listening to the bombardment and waiting for news of whether the fort would hold.

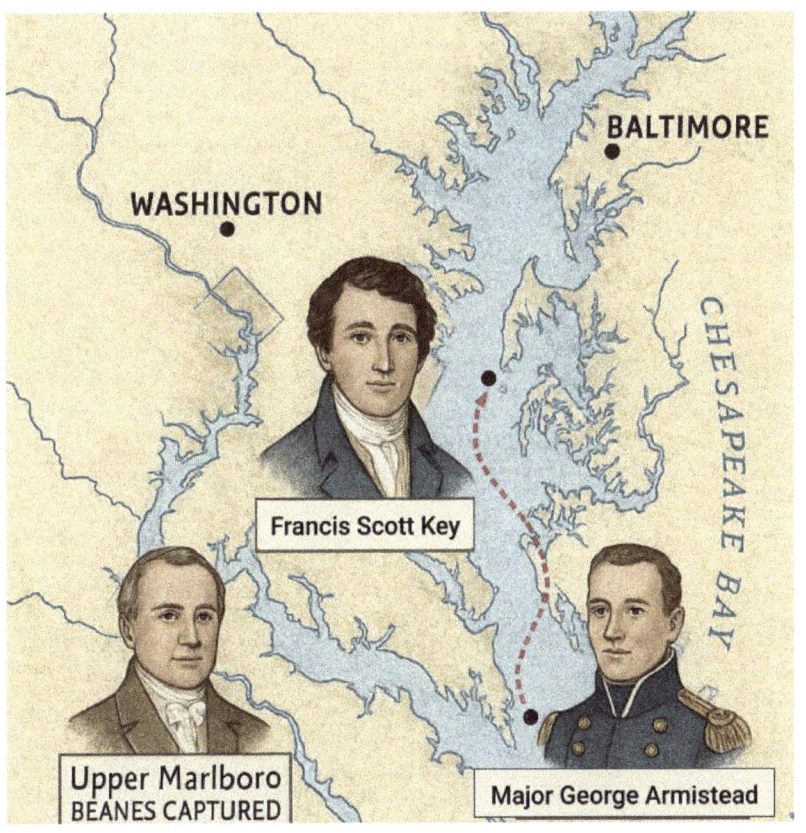

Line 6: "Gave proof through the night that our flag was still there

Here, Key explains why the rockets and bombs mattered. Each explosion in the night sky gave him evidence—proof—that the American flag was still flying. Even without daylight, he could see it. This line transforms symbols of war into symbols of hope.

The idea of "proof" is powerful. In the dark uncertainty of battle, people long for a sign that their side is still fighting. For Key, seeing the flag through bursts of light gave reassurance that America had not surrendered. It also suggested that the defenders inside Fort McHenry were determined to resist no matter what.

This line highlights the way people look for signs of survival in hard times. The flag became more than just cloth—it became living proof of freedom holding on through the storm of war.

The Flag was still There!

The massive flag Mary Pickersgill had sewn was critical in providing that "proof." Its size—30 by 42 feet—made it visible even in the dim flashes of explosions. Major Armistead's decision to commission such a large flag turned out to be an act of foresight and symbolism.

During the night, the smaller "storm flags" were raised to protect the larger garrison flag from damage in heavy winds and rain. However, by dawn, Armistead ordered the great flag raised once more, ensuring that when the smoke cleared, the British would see an unmistakable sign of defiance.

Baltimore's citizens also looked for proof. From rooftops and hills, people watched the bombardment, straining to catch glimpses of the fort's flag. If the flag fell, they feared the city would be lost. Instead, the sight of the banner reassured both Key and Baltimoreans that their defenders still held out.

Line 7: "O say does that star-spangled banner yet wave"

In this line, Key again asks the central question: is the flag still waving? Even after describing the night's events, his words still carry suspense. The anthem is built on this tension—only at the end the answer will be fully revealed. The repetition of the question also reflects Key's anxiety. He had spent the entire night watching, waiting, and wondering. It wasn't until dawn's first full light that he could know for sure. This line places the listener right in that moment of uncertainty alongside him.

For Key, this line shows how deeply symbols matter. Key's focus wasn't on numbers of soldiers or cannons—it was on the flag. The flag represented the spirit of the nation, and if it still waved, America was still alive and free.

The Star-Spangled Banner

The phrase "star-spangled banner" refers to the American flag, covered with stars to represent the states and stripes for the original thirteen colonies. By 1814, the flag had 15 stars and 15 stripes, representing the expanded nation.

From his ship in the Patapsco River, Key had no way to communicate with the fort. He could only ask himself, and by extension the nation: Does the star-spangled banner still wave? His words captured not only his own suspense but the uncertainty of an entire young nation.

Line 8: "O'er the land of the free and the home of the brave?"

Finally, Key ties the survival of the flag to the survival of the nation. If the flag is still there, it waves not just over Fort McHenry but over all of America—the "land of the free and the home of the brave." The line is both a question and a declaration: America will remain free, as long as its people are brave enough to defend it.

The phrase "land of the free" emphasizes liberty, the ideal for which Americans fought in both the Revolutionary War and now again in the War of 1812. The phrase "home of the brave" honors the courage of the defenders at Fort McHenry who risked their lives to keep the flag flying. Together, freedom and bravery are shown as inseparable.

This line sums up the anthem's message: freedom is not free—it is defended by brave people, and it survives when ordinary citizens stand up in extraordinary times.

The War of 1812 was often called the "Second War of Independence." Britain still saw America as a former colony rather than a fully equal nation. American sailors were being captured at sea, and British troops had burned the capital. Baltimore's defense symbolized that America would not be reabsorbed into British power.

The geography of Baltimore made it a key port city. If Britain had succeeded in taking Fort McHenry, their navy could have sailed into the harbor and captured Baltimore, cutting off trade and striking a devastating blow. Instead, the bravery of the defenders preserved the city—and by extension, the nation's morale.

Key's words also reflected the growing American identity. The United States was only 38 years old at the time. Calling it the "land of the free and the home of the brave" gave the young nation a motto that combined values (freedom) and character (bravery). These ideals would echo throughout American history, making this final line one of the most memorable patriotic phrases ever written.

Verses Two through Four

As the national anthem, most people don't know of verses two through four. In fact, as you read them you will not be able to align them with the anthem's well known, however non-typical, melodic orchestration—it was written as a poem with four verses.

Francis Scott Key originally wrote The Star-Spangled Banner as a poem in September 1814, titled "The Defence of Fort M'Henry." It wasn't written with music in mind.

Soon after, the words were set to the tune of a popular British song called "To Anacreon in Heaven." It was the official song of the Anacreontic Society, a London gentlemen's music club. The melody was already well-known in America by 1814 and often used for patriotic or drinking songs.

Because the melody fit the rhythm and meter of Key's poem, it quickly caught on. Within weeks, newspapers printed the poem with instructions to sing it to the tune of "To Anacreon in Heaven." That combination of words and music spread, and over time, it became the patriotic anthem we know today.

So, as you read on to the next verses, forget about the melody so closely associated with the anthem, and read them as you would a poetic tribute to our nation.

Verse 2

On the shore dimly seen through the mists of the deep,

Where the foe's haughty host in dread silence reposes,

What is that which the breeze, o'er the towering steep,

As it fitfully blows, half conceals, half discloses?

Now it catches the gleam of the morning's first beam,

In full glory reflected now shines in the stream:

'Tis the star-spangled banner! O long may it wave

O'er the land of the free and the home of the brave.

This verse shifts from night to dawn. Through the mist, Key describes the enemy fleet lying silently at anchor. The British had bombarded all night but failed to take the fort. As morning arrives, Key sees the flag emerge clearly in the breeze.

The language of concealment and disclosure—half conceals, half discloses—mirrors the tension of waiting through the night. Finally, the morning sun breaks through, and the flag appears in "full glory." The relief is overwhelming: the banner is still flying.

The verse ends as a prayerful hope: may the flag "long wave" as a symbol of freedom and bravery for the nation.

At dawn on September 14, the British realized their bombardment had failed to force Fort McHenry's surrender. The fleet lay silently beyond the harbor, having exhausted their strategy. Baltimore's defenses—sunken ships, chains, and artillery—had kept them from sailing closer. They could not approach and could not invade the shoreline.

The "towering steep" refers to the walls of Fort McHenry itself, which rose above the waters of the Patapsco River. From Key's ship, the fort would have been partially obscured by mist and smoke. The breeze revealed the flag in flashes until sunlight finally confirmed it was still there.

This sight was more than military news—it was psychological victory. Washington, D.C. had just been burned by the British three weeks earlier. Baltimore's survival proved America could withstand the world's most powerful navy.

Verse 3

And where is that band who so vauntingly swore

That the havoc of war and the battle's confusion,

A home and a country, should leave us no more?

Their blood has washed out their foul footsteps' pollution.

No refuge could save the hireling and slave

From the terror of flight, or the gloom of the grave:

And the star-spangled banner in triumph doth wave,

O'er the land of the free and the home of the brave.

This verse is more defiant. Key mocks the British soldiers who swore America would be destroyed. Instead, their boast has failed. He suggests that their "pollution" has been cleansed by their own blood spilled in battle.

The verse also points out that neither mercenaries ("hirelings") nor enslaved people promised freedom for fighting with the British ("slaves") were able to escape defeat. The central theme: those who attack America will fail, while the flag of freedom and bravery triumphs.

This verse is more controversial because of its reference to slavery. It reflects the complex and often troubling realities of early 19th-century America.

The British had recruited both mercenary troops (from Germany and elsewhere) and enslaved African Americans who were promised freedom if they fought for Britain. This verse reflects Key's disdain for those forces.

Baltimore was defended not only by soldiers but by citizen militias determined to protect their homes. British overconfidence—vauntingly swore—had led them to underestimate American resolve. The Battle of Baltimore proved that even after the humiliation of Washington's burning, Americans could rally and resist.

Geographically, the British fleet began retreating after the bombardment. Their land attack had already been stopped at the Battle of North Point. Verse 3 celebrates this as a turning point where British aggression was beaten back.

Verse 4

O thus be it ever, when freemen shall stand

Between their loved home and the war's desolation!

Blest with vict'ry and peace, may the Heav'n rescued land

Praise the Power that hath made and preserved us a nation.

Then conquer we must, when our cause it is just,

And this be our motto: "In God is our trust."

And the star-spangled banner in triumph shall wave

O'er the land of the free and the home of the brave!

This final verse moves from description to prayer. Key writes that whenever free people stand to defend their homes against destruction, God will bless their land with victory and peace. He praises divine providence for preserving the young United States as a nation.

The verse also declares a motto: "In God is our trust." This idea would echo through American history, eventually inspiring the U.S. national motto, "In God We Trust." The anthem closes on a triumphant note: as long as Americans are just and brave, the star-spangled banner will continue to wave over their free land.

In 1814, America was still fragile. The War of 1812 had divided the country politically, and military defeats had shaken morale. Baltimore's defense was seen as proof that God favored the United States and its survival.

This verse highlights the religious worldview of the time. Many Americans saw the war as a test of the nation's legitimacy. If God preserved them against mighty Britain, it proved their cause was just.

The phrase "In God is our trust" eventually became part of American culture and identity. It later appeared on U.S. coins during the Civil War (1864) and was officially declared the national motto in 1956.

The triumph of Fort McHenry was not just a battle won—it became a symbol of America's ability to defend itself, guided by faith, bravery, and determination.

Dedication

To the Class of 2030 and beyond (today's middle-schoolers)—

    This book is dedicated to you, the rising generation of American young people who will soon inherit the blessings of freedom and the responsibilities that come with it.

    Take each opportunity to remove your hat, place your hand over your heart, proudly, and sing with full voice, feeling the patriotism and pride of being an American.

    It is my hope and dream that as you sing The Star-Spangled Banner, you do so with understanding—knowing that the anthem is not just a song, but a story of courage, sacrifice, and deliverance.

    A story written by a real person, about a real battle, where shots were fired, blood spilled, and lives lost—on both sides—for a dream.

    May you always remember the grave price so many have paid in service to our country, our flag, and the freedoms it represents.

    May these words inspire you to stand tall, to honor the past, and to carry forward the spirit of patriotism with which our anthem was written.

— For America's youth, today and always

www.ingramcontent.com/pod-product-compliance
Lightning Source LLC
Chambersburg PA
CBHW050735010526
44107CB00010B/856